SCHOLASTIC

Grades 3–6

25 Totally Terrific Science Projects

Easy How-to's and Templates for Projects That Motivate Students to Show What They Know About Key Science Topics

MICHAEL GRAVOIS

New York • Toronto • London • Auckland • Sydney
Mexico City • New Delhi • Hong Kong • Buenos Aires

Teaching *Resources*

Dedication

To Carol Wolder

Each friend represents a world in us,
a world possibly not born until they arrive,
and it is only by this meeting that a new world is born.
—Anaïs Nin

Cover design by Maria Lilja
Interior design by Michael Gravois
Illustrations by Teresa Anderko
Photographs by Jason Robinson, except pages 13, 38, and 76 by Maria Lilja;
page 59 photo © David Woods/Shutterstock

ISBN-13: 978-0-545-23139-8
ISBN-10: 0-545-23139-6

Contents

Contents

Physical Science

Introduction

About the Book

Everywhere we look, we can find science—from the heating systems that keep our classrooms warm on a winter's day to the meals cooking in the school cafeteria, from the class recycling bin to the change of seasons outside the window, from the school's landscaping to the health of our students. Scientific discoveries and technological advances are transforming our lives at an ever-increasing pace, and it is up to us as teachers to groom and cultivate our future astronomers, zoologists, environmentalists, and chemists.

Isaac Asimov, the great writer of science fiction novels and popular science books, once said, "The most exciting phrase to hear in science, the one that heralds new discoveries, is not 'Eureka!' but 'That's funny . . .'" This seed of curiosity is the one that creates a classroom filled with self-motivated scientists. The projects in this book are meant to help you teach science concepts in a fun, hands-on way, making your lessons unique and varied, and engaging your students in their learning. Using these activities, you'll have your students adding "That's fun!" to the phrase "That's funny . . ."

How to Use the Book

This book is divided into four main sections—

General Science   Life Science

Earth Science   Physical Science

Though the projects in each section relate to specific topics, they can easily be shifted to another category or adapted to

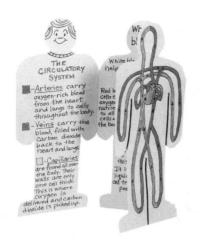

meet your needs. You'll also find helpful advice under the Teacher Tip icon in the sidebars that describe time-saving techniques, display ideas, and ways in which the projects can be used for different purposes.

The materials you will need for each project are listed in the sidebar underneath the project's title. The majority of the materials are common supplies that can be found in most classrooms.

The projects in the book help students develop science skills and were adapted from a variety of national and state science standards. The skills and standards related to each project are listed in the sidebar below the materials list.

Many of the projects also include ready-to-go templates and reproducibles to help students complete their work. So, look through the book and explore the possibilities.

Best of all, you can use the ideas in this book to keep the school days interesting, challenging, and fun, and create an environment where curiosity thrives.

Student Assessment

Grading should not be some mysterious cipher for students to unravel. Rather, it is our duty as teachers to provide clear expectations about what will be assessed, concepts and skills that need to be mastered, performance standards that should be achieved, and where the student's strengths and weaknesses lie. Therefore, we must develop assessment tools—like rubrics—to provide a coherent reference that allows students to know exactly what is expected of them and enables them to achieve the best possible grade.

As you develop rubrics for the projects in this book, determine which skills and standards you are assessing so you can chart each student's understanding of the material. Also consider which qualities of the process (time management, organization, following instructions, communication with teacher and/or classmates) and product (spelling, grammar, punctuation, neatness, presentation) you will be assessing.

Once you've set the assessment criteria, review the rubric with your students when you assign the project. This gives them a reference by which they can plot their progress and produce their best work.

People Book

Materials:
- colored pencils
- scissors
- glue sticks
- white construction paper

Skills/Standards:
- understands the nature of scientific knowledge
- researches the three main branches of science—life, earth, and physical sciences
- identifies traits, characteristics, and attributes of different scientific jobs

Teacher Tip

Provide an assortment of craft items, such as buttons, feathers, glitter, and dimensional glue, for the students to use when decorating their people books.

Purpose

Students will investigate a variety of scientific careers and create a people book that highlights the educational path and job responsibilities of a chosen profession.

Creating the People Book

1. Give each student a sheet of white construction paper and have them fold it in half horizontally twice and then once vertically. When opened, it will reveal eight panels.

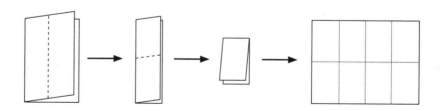

2. Ask students to cut the bottom left and bottom right panels as indicated below and set the scraps aside to use later. Then have students make a slit up the center to create pants.

General Science

Students can read biographies and create people books of famous scientists like Jacques Cousteau, Marie Curie, Isaac Newton, Carl Sagan, and Dian Fossey. After students have completed their reports, staple the arms and legs of the people books to a bulletin board. Add a banner that says Wonder Is the Seed of Science.

Earth Science

Every student can create a people book that looks like an astronaut. Inside it, they can write about aspects of space travel, planets, or objects found in space. Add the people books, planets, stars, and a space station to a bulletin board covered in dark blue paper for an out of this world display!

3. Have students fold in the top left and top right panels. Then ask them to glue the two scraps behind the top two panels to create sleeves.

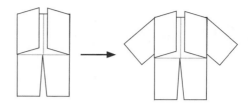

4. Instruct students to cut a head, hands, and feet from another sheet of paper and add them to the figure.

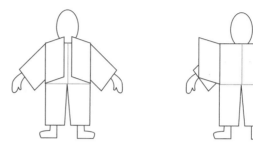

Completing the People Book

1. Have students use colored pencils to draw clothing or a uniform that is characteristic of the scientific field their figure represents.

2. Ask students to use construction paper to create an object to put in the scientist's hand that is relevant to his or her field of work.

3. Inside the two flaps that cover the chest, have students write two detailed paragraphs that describe the educational path and responsibilities of the scientist.

4. Encourage students to prepare an oral report on this scientist to present to the class.

Suggested List of Scientific Fields

anthropologist	cytologist	geophysicist	meteorologist	physicist
archeologist	ecologist	glaciologist	microbiologist	physiologist
astronomer	entomologist	herpetologist	minerologist	psychologist
astrophysicist	environmentalist	horticulturalist	nanotechnologist	seismologist
biochemist	etymologist	hydrophysicist	neuroscientist	sociologist
biologist	gemologist	ichthyologist	oceanographer	toxicologist
botanist	genealogist	lepidopterist	ornithologist	virologist
chemist	geneticist	limnologist	paleontologist	volcanologist
computer scientist	geologist	linguist	pharmacologist	zoologist

Vocabulary Book

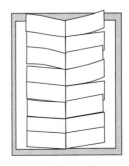

Materials:

- colored pencils
- scissors
- glue sticks
- 12- by 9-inch sheets of construction paper
- Vocabulary Strips template (page 10)

Skills/Standards:

- builds science vocabulary
- explores science concepts

General Science

Students can write a date on the front of each flap and then lift the flap to write about the significance of the date. For example, students could track the history of indoor illumination (from sunlight and torches, to oil lamps, to gas lamps, to electricity). Or they can create a time line of the space program, the life of a scientist, or the impact certain inventions have had on humankind.

Purpose

Students will learn vocabulary words and terms related to a science concept they are studying.

Creating the Vocabulary Book

1. Give each student a 12- by 9-inch sheet of construction paper and two copies of the Vocabulary Strips template. Ask students to fold all three sheets in half vertically; the *blank* side of the templates should be on the inside of the fold.

2. Have students open both templates and cut along the dashed lines, stopping at the center line crease. This will create eight tabs on each sheet (figure 1).

3. Tell students to glue the back of the uncut side of one template to the inside left cover of the construction paper. Repeat using the other template for the inside right cover. The center folds of the templates should touch the center fold of the construction paper and the flaps should face out (figure 2).

4. Students can write a different vocabulary word on each of the 16 tabs. Then they can lift each tab and write the word's definition beneath it. Ask students to close their vocabulary books and use creative lettering to write a title.

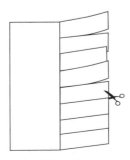

figure 1

figure 2

Blossom Book

Materials:

- wooden skewers
- colored pencils
- glue sticks
- scissors
- tape
- card stock
- green construction paper
- 8½- by 11-inch pastel-colored copy paper

Skills/Standards:

- develops an understanding of plant life
- collects and organizes information from multiple sources
- recognizes relationships between plants and animals
- builds science vocabulary

Teacher Tip

To save class time, show students how to fold one of the squares and then have them fold the other two and enter the information for homework. Then students could construct the blossom books in class.

Purpose

Students will create a blossom book that features information they learned about the world of plants—the parts of a flower, necessities for plant growth, methods of seed dispersal, the relationships between plants and animals, and so on.

Creating the Blossom Book

1. Give each student three sheets of pastel-colored copy paper. Ask students to pull the top left corner of one sheet down diagonally to the right so that the top edge of the paper aligns with the right edge of the paper. Crease along the fold (figure 1). Then have them cut off the bottom strip of paper so that they are left with an 8½-inch square (figure 2).

2. Have students place the square in front of them so the crease is "mountain-side" up (rather than "valley-side" up). Students should fold the square in half vertically, crease it, and open it. They then fold it in half horizontally, crease it, and open it. When opened, the paper will have three creases (figure 3).

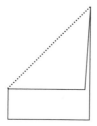

figure 1

figure 2

figure 3

Life Science

Experiment with cutting the blossom book in different ways. For example, if you are studying the circulatory system, use red paper and cut the folded squares into the shape of a heart.

Physical Science

Since blossom books contain three pages, they're a great way for students to compare and contrast three things, such as the properties of solids, liquids, and gases. However, a fourth or fifth page can be added for a longer, more detailed blossom book.

3. Ask students to repeat these steps for all three pieces of copy paper.

4. Then have students fold one of the pieces of paper in half along the diagonal crease (figure 4). They should push points A and B into the inside to point C (figure 5), making a smaller square (figure 6). They can now do this to all three pages.

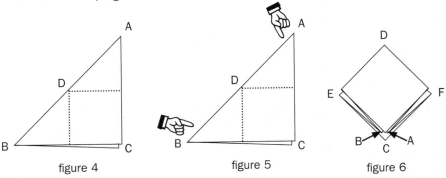

figure 4   figure 5   figure 6

5. Have students place one of the folded squares in front of them with the open side, point C, at the bottom. Instruct them to draw a clover-shaped outline on the square, starting midway between points E and D and ending midway between points F and D (figure 7).

6. Ask students to cut along the line they just drew, making sure to cut through all the layers of the folded paper (figure 8).

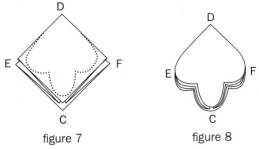

figure 7   figure 8

7. Have students use the shape they just cut as a template to draw a matching clover-shaped outline on the other two folded squares. They should then cut the other two squares along the lines they just drew.

8. Next, students should place one of the folded shapes onto a sheet of card stock and trace around the shape. Have them cut out this shape and repeat this step so they end up with two clover-shaped pieces of card stock. Students may set these aside for the moment. The pieces will be used later to form the front and back cover of the blossom book.

Completing the Blossom Book

1. Instruct students to open the three folded shapes. Within the blooms, students can draw and write information regarding plants and flowers that they've researched and studied. For example, students can illustrate and label the parts of a flower, write sentences describing the parts of a flower, illustrate methods of seed dispersal, or chart the growth of a seed they've planted in a paper cup.

2. After students have recorded the information, instruct them to refold the paper as before and stack the three shapes on top of each other, making sure to line up point D on all three pages.

3. Ask students to glue the bottom of shape 1 to the top of shape 2. Then they should glue the bottom of shape 2 to the top of shape 3.

4. Have students tape a wooden skewer to the top and bottom of the folded shapes so it sticks out beyond point C (figure 9).

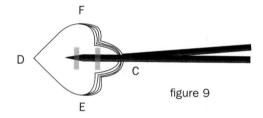

figure 9

5. Students can then glue the two pieces of card stock to each side of the blossom book, covering the wooden skewers. To open the blossom book, pull the skewers apart and around so that the front and back covers meet.

6. Ask students to cut two leaves from green construction paper and tape them to the two skewers. Have students write a title for the blossom book on one of the leaves and their name on the other leaf.

Earth Science

A blossom book can be cut into a circular shape, as shown below. Just make sure you leave a part of each edge connected. Each folded page will blossom into four connected circles. When you attach three pages together, there are twelve circles on which students can write information, perfect for reporting on the planets and objects in the solar system.

Teacher Tip

If you would like to display the blossom books, open them up and stick the skewers into blocks of floral foam or clay. Line them up on a shelf or table top.

Step Book

Materials:
- stapler
- colored pencils
- rulers
- pencils
- scissors
- 8½- by 11-inch copy paper

Skills/Standards:
- understands the nature of scientific inquiry
- knows that animal life can be classified based on common traits
- identifies different ways in which living things can be grouped
- identifies traits, characteristics, or attributes of animals
- organizes and interprets data
- develops critical-thinking skills

Teacher Tip

For an easier-to-make step book, just fold the pages as shown in figures 1 and 2 at right. Or you could use two or three pages for a book with fewer panels.

Purpose

Students will create a step book to help them organize and classify animal life by kingdom, phylum, class, order, family, genus, and species.

Creating the Step Book

1. Give each student four sheets of 8½- by 11-inch copy paper.

2. Have students lay the four sheets on top of each other so that ¾-inch strips of the back pages show at the bottom (figure 1).

3. Ask students to bend the tops of the pages backward (figure 2) to reveal ¾-inch strips of panels 5, 6, 7, and 8 (figure 3). Fasten the top with two staples.

4. On the bottom strip, panel 8, have students draw a light vertical line 1¼ inches from the left edge (figure 4).

5. Ask students to cut away the strip to the right of the vertical line they just drew (figure 5).

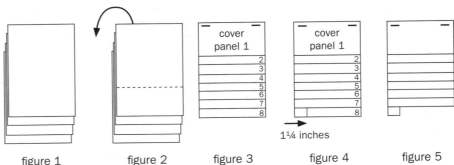

figure 1   figure 2   figure 3   figure 4   figure 5

6. On the second to last strip, panel 7, have students draw a light vertical line 2½ inches from the left edge. Ask them to cut away the strips on panels 7 and 8 that are to the right of this vertical line (figure 6).

7. On panels 6, 5, 4, and 3, students should draw a line 3¾ inches, 5 inches, 6¼ inches, and 7½ inches, respectively, from the left edge. They should cut away *all* the strips to the right of each of these lines to create a "stepped" look to the strips (figure 7).

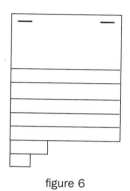

figure 6

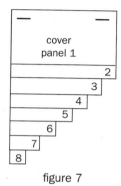

figure 7

Completing the Step Book

1. On the cover panel, ask students to use creative lettering to write a title, such as "Amelia's Step Book of the Animal Kingdom."

2. On the smallest strip at the bottom, panel 8, ask students to write the title "Species."

3. On the right side of panel 7, students should write the title "Genus."

4. On each of the other strips, ask students to write—in ascending order—the titles "Family," "Order," "Class," "Phylum," and "Kingdom." (See photo of final project on page 14.)

5. Ask students to lift the cover panel to reveal panel 2. On the underside of the cover panel, instruct students to write a definition of the term "Kingdom." Then have them use creative lettering to write the word "Animalia," which is the type of kingdom they will be researching. In the area above the title strip for this panel, ask students to list the names of a variety of animals (see example on page 16). This list should include vertebrates, invertebrates, mammals, reptiles, insects, birds, and so on.

General Science

On each of the panels, ask students to record and discuss the steps in a scientific experiment.

Physical Science

On each tab, students can write the chemical formulas of different molecules. They can illustrate the molecules on each of the panels.

6. Have students lift panel 2 to reveal panel 3. On the underside of panel 2, students should write a definition for the term "Phylum." Then have them use creative lettering to write a word describing a type of phylum—such as "Chordata," which are animals that are vertebrates or one of several closely related invertebrates. In the area above the title strip for this panel, ask students to list all the animals from the first list that are a part of this phylum.

7. Instruct students to lift panel 3 to reveal panel 4. On the underside of panel 3, students should write a definition for the term "Class," then use creative lettering to write a word describing a type of class—such as "Mammalia," which are animals that are mammals. In the area above the title strip for this panel, have students list all the animals that are a part of this class.

8. Students should continue refining the list on each of the succeeding panels until they are left with the species name of one of the animals from the original list. Encourage them to draw a picture of the chosen animal on this panel.

Desk Tree

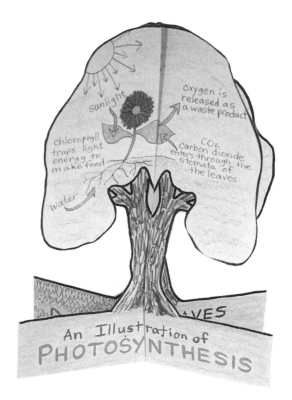

Materials:
- colored pencils
- scissors
- rulers
- 8½- by 11-inch card stock
- Desk Tree template (page 19)

Skills/Standards:
- develops an understanding of plant life
- understands the nature of scientific inquiry
- organizes and interprets data
- recognizes the relationship between plants and animals
- understands the concept of photosynthesis and the function of chlorophyll

Physical Science

The teacher can conduct an experiment that explores chemical and physical changes of trees—forest fires, rainstorms, making furniture—by burning, wetting, and breaking a matchstick. Students can write about their observations on their desk tree.

Purpose

Students will create a desk tree that features information they learned about the world of trees and plants—the process of photosynthesis, reasons why trees change colors, the function of chlorophyll, and so on.

Creating the Desk Tree

1. Give each student two sheets of 8½- by 11-inch card stock and a copy of the Desk Tree template.

2. Have students cut out the tree's silhouette along the dotted line on the reproducible.

3. Ask students to use the silhouette as a template and trace it onto both sheets of card stock. They should then cut out both silhouettes from the card stock.

4. Direct students to place the template behind one of the pieces of card stock and hold it up to a window; this allows them to faintly see the dashed center line on the template. Have them lightly trace the center line onto the card stock; they should also mark where the two black circles are.

5. On one of the silhouettes, students should cut from the bottom of the center line up to the top circle. On the other, they should cut from the top of the center line down to the bottom circle.

Life Science

Assign a different species of tree to each student. Ask students to find a silhouette of their tree on the Internet and create a desk tree of their assigned tree. Students can write about the habitat in which their tree can be found, illustrate its leaf, describe its fruit or flower, or create a time line of its lifespan. They might also compare monocots to dicots or coniferous trees to deciduous trees.

Earth Science

Students can illustrate and describe the affect the Earth's revolution has upon seasonal changes. Each of the four panels on the desk tree can address a different season.

6. Show students how to slide the two silhouettes together so they lock into place (figure 1). The bottom edges of the two silhouettes need to line up so the tree can stand freely. There will be four tree-shaped panels on which the students can write or draw.

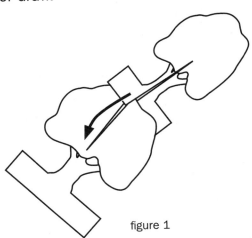

figure 1

Completing the Desk Tree

1. Once the trees are interlocked, ask students to lay them down on their desk; the tree will naturally lie flat. Ask students to write a title for their desk tree and include their name. Encourage students to color the tree, adding leaves and bark.

2. Students need only turn the pages to reveal each of the other three panels. Direct students to fill in the required information on these panels; information can include a definition of photosynthesis and chlorophyll, an illustration of the photosynthetic process, a paragraph describing why trees change colors, and so on. Ask students to write a title for each panel on the strip below the silhouettes.

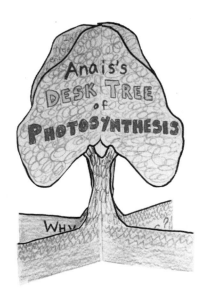

Template **Desk Tree**

Cycle Card

Materials:

- colored pencils
- scissors
- rulers
- glue sticks
- 8½- by 11-inch card stock

Skills/Standards:

- gathers and uses information for research purposes
- understands the organization of simple food chains
- knows how organisms interact and depend on one another through food chains
- explores how energy is transferred through food chains in an ecosystem
- understands cause and effect relationships

Teacher Tip

When students measure and draw lines, such as the ones in step 2 at the right, encourage them to make three marks when measuring. If one of the marks is measured incorrectly, it becomes apparent when they lay down the ruler to draw the line.

Purpose

Students will create a cycle card that explores the cyclical effect of a food chain and the interdependence of plants and animals for their continued growth and survival.

Creating the Cycle Card

1. Give each student two sheets of 8½- by 11-inch card stock.

2. Have students lay the card stock in front of them horizontally. Instruct students to draw a line 4¼ inches from the left edge and another line 8½ inches from the left edge (figure 1). They should do this to both sheets.

3. Ask students to cut along these lines so they have four sheets of card stock that measure 4¼ by 8½. They can discard the two thin strips.

4. Students should lay these four sheets in front of them horizontally and draw a line 2⅛ inches from the left edge of each sheet and another line 2⅛ inches from the right edge of each sheet (figure 2).

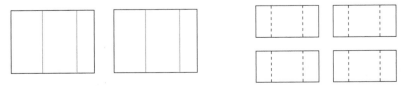

figure 1   figure 2

5. Ask students to fold all four sheets along both lines so the edges meet in the center. The edges should not overlap. If they do, students should trim them a little. Have students reopen the sheets.

6. Instruct students to fold two of the pieces in half horizontally (figure 3). Students should fold and unfold all of the creases so they are pliable.

7. Have students lay the two pieces they just folded–one above the other–so the bottom edge of one abuts the top edge of the other (figure 4).

8. Students should put glue in the four corners, making sure not to let it go over the score lines (figure 5).

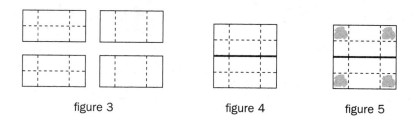

figure 3   figure 4   figure 5

9. Ask students to lay the other two sheets of card stock on top of the sheets that have glue on them, attaching them one corner at a time (figure 6). The cycle card is now ready to be decorated (figure 7).

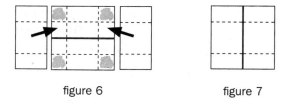

figure 6   figure 7

Completing the Cycle Card

1. Students should pick a biome (such as a pond, a rain forest, a desert, or a coniferous forest—as is shown in the sample project). They will create a cycle card that examines a simple food chain found in the biome they selected.

2. On the cover, students should use creative lettering to write the title Producers. They should draw a picture of producers

Life Science

A cycle card is a fascinating way to document the metamorphic life cycle of frogs, butterflies, and cicadas, or to report on the circulation of blood through the human body.

Physical Science

The biochemical cycles of elements such as oxygen, carbon, sulfur, and nitrogen can be examined and recorded using cycle cards.

Students can illustrate and describe a different season on each of the four panels of a cycle card, or they can chart the repeating steps of the water cycle.

found in the chosen biome and write a couple of sentences about them, describing their role in the food chain (figure 8).

3. Students should open the center of the cover panel to reveal the second panel (figure 9). On this panel, they should write about herbivores found in the biome and draw a related picture. (Note: The sides of this panel can also be seen when the third panel is revealed; remind students to take this into account when drawing the picture.)

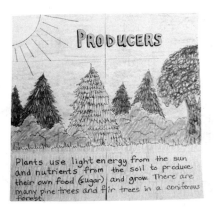

figure 8

figure 9

4. Show students how to lift the center of the second panel to reveal the third panel (figure 10). On this panel, they should write about carnivores found in the biome and draw a related picture.

5. Students should open the center of the third panel to reveal the fourth panel (figure 11). On this panel, they should write about the role of decomposers found in the biome and draw a related picture.

6. Students can open the fourth panel to reveal the cover panel, cycling through the neverending process of the food chain.

figure 10

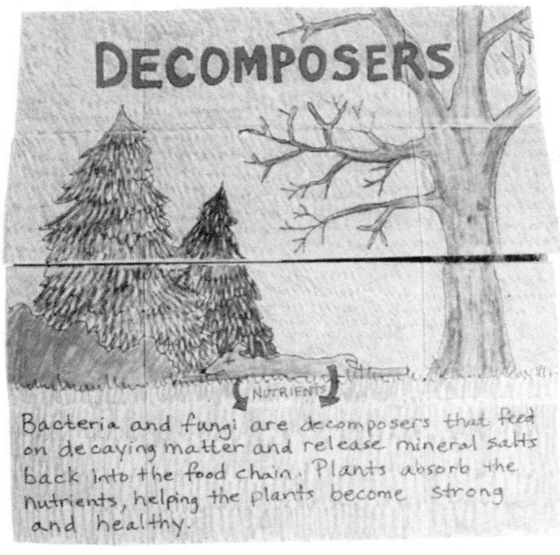

figure 11

Tunnel Book

Materials:
- colored pencils
- glue sticks
- scissors
- ruler
- 8½- by 11-inch card stock
- utility knife (for teacher use only)

Skills/Standards:
- identifies characteristics of an ecosystem
- recognizes relationships between organisms and their physical environment
- knows that an ecosystem is all populations living together and the physical factors they interact with
- understands that all organisms, including humans, cause changes in their environment, and that these changes can be beneficial or detrimental

Purpose

Students will design a tunnel book that depicts an animal in its natural habitat and describes its relationship to the ecosystem in which it lives.

Creating the Tunnel Book

1. Give each student four sheets of 8½- by 11-inch card stock.

2. Have students create a 1-inch border around three sheets of card stock. Within the border of one sheet, ask students to draw and color the background of an ecosystem in which an animal of their choosing can be found. In the example above, you can see a background that depicts a rain forest. On the backside of this picture, ask students to write a paragraph that describes the ecosystem and an animal that can be found in this ecosystem. The paragraph should have a 1½-inch border on the left and right sides.

3. Within the border of a second sheet, students should draw and color the mid-ground (middle layer), which depicts an animal that lives in that ecosystem. The animal and environmental elements should be connected to the border. In the example above, you can see a parrot and vines in the mid-ground layer. Students should cut out all of the white space around the colored elements. To help them get started, use a utility knife to cut a small *X* in each of the white areas, through which students can stick their scissors.

When studying prehistoric eras, have students create tunnel books of what the Earth might have looked like during these fascinating times.

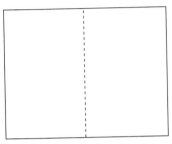

4. Within the border of the third sheet, students should draw and color the foreground (front layer), which depicts a few environmental elements of the ecosystem. The foreground should be drawn in a way that allows the animal in the mid-ground to be seen once they cut away the uncolored areas. In the example on page 23, you can see some leaves and vines in the foreground layer. Instruct students to cut away the white space around the colored elements.

5. Ask students to cut the fourth sheet of card stock in half so they have two sheets that measure 8½ by 5½ inches (figure 1).

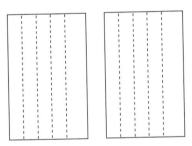

figure 1

6. Have students lay these two sheets vertically in front of them and draw four lines that are each one inch apart, starting from the left side of the sheets (figure 2). The far right strips will measure 1½ inches.

figure 2

7. Show students how to fold both sheets along these lines so they form an S pattern (figure 3). Students can lay a ruler along each line as they fold the card stock to make it easier to form the creases.

8. Ask students to stand the two bent pieces of card stock in front of them so the 1½-inch strips line up in the back (figure 3).

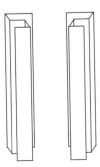

figure 3

Completing the Tunnel Book

1. Have students put glue on the sides of the paragraph they wrote and attach it to the front side of the 1½-inch strips.

2. Have them rub glue on the right and left border to the sides of the mid-ground layer and attach it to the 1-inch panel that faces the background layer.

3. Finally, have students rub glue on the back of the side borders of the foreground layer and attach it to the 1-inch panel at the front (figure 4).

Life Science

Create a class zoo that features animals found in your state, or create a bunch of aquariums that teem with aquatic life.

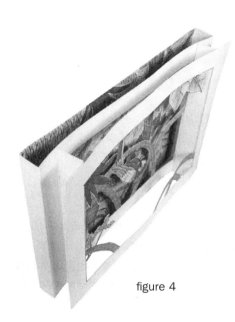

figure 4

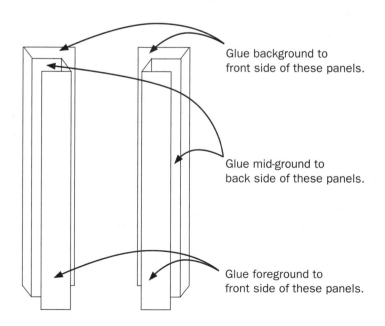

Glue background to front side of these panels.

Glue mid-ground to back side of these panels.

Glue foreground to front side of these panels.

Wisdom Tent

Bighorn Sheep can be found in the western United States and Canada.

Materials:
- colored pencils
- glue sticks
- Wisdom Tent template (page 28)

Skills/Standards:
- understands the nature of scientific inquiry
- gathers and uses information for research purposes
- knows that changes in the environment can have different effects on different organisms
- knows that all organisms (including humans) cause changes in their environments, and these changes can be beneficial or detrimental

Physical Science

Students can create a pair of wisdom tents that explain the differences between potential and kinetic energy.

General Science

Students can create three wisdom tents, each of which focuses on a different branch of science.

Purpose

Students will conduct simple research assignments to learn why certain animals have become endangered.

Creating the Wisdom Tent

1. Give each student a copy of the Wisdom Tent template. On the lines at the bottom of the page, ask students to write a paragraph about an endangered animal, including information about how it became endangered and what can be done to help its survival.

2. Then have students spin the paper around so the paragraph is upside down and draw a picture of the animal within the frame. To the left of the drawing, students should use creative lettering to write the name of the animal and the area or areas in which the animal can be found.

3. Next, have students fold the paper along the dashed line, making sure the writing is on the outside of the fold (figure 1).

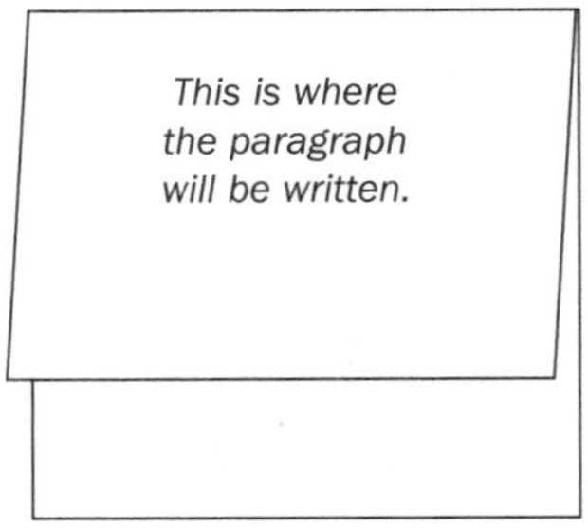

This is where the paragraph will be written.

figure 1

4. Using the edge of the paper beneath the paragraph as a guide, have students fold the bottom panel upward so the words *Template: Wisdom Tent* are visible (figure 2).

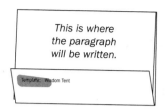

figure 2

5. Instruct students to make a quarter inch fold on this bottom panel and glue it to the back of the panel that has the paragraph (figures 3 and 4). The wisdom tent can now stand freely on the students's desks or on a classroom counter.

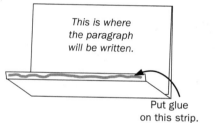

Put glue on this strip.

figure 3

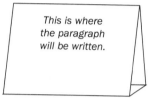

figure 4

Earth Science

Create a list of different landforms. Ask each student to pick a landform and create a wisdom tent that illustrates it and describes how it is formed.

Life Science

Have students work in groups in which each member creates a wisdom tent that focuses on a different body system.

Teacher Tip

Wisdom tents also make great greeting cards that can stand on their own. Simply fold the bottom flap upward, flatten the card, and insert it into an envelope. Use card stock for added durability.

Template **Wisdom Tent**

Body Brochure

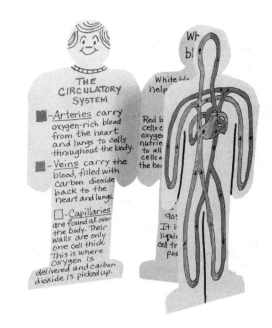

Materials:
- colored pencils
- scissors
- Body Brochure template (page 31)

Skills/Standards:
- understands the nature of scientific inquiry
- collects and organizes information from multiple sources
- investigates major systems of the human body
- identifies anatomical makeup of different body systems

Teacher Tip

Create a crowd-pleasing display by stapling the inside center panel of the brochure to a bulletin board. Viewers can easily open the panels to read the information inside.

Purpose

Students will create a trifold brochure that contains information they learned about one of the major systems of the human body.

Creating the Body Brochure

1. Give each student a copy of the Body Brochure template. (When you make copies, cover the header and footer with a small piece of white paper so they don't appear.)

2. Have students turn the template over so the silhouette is on the back. Ask them to fold the paper into a trifold brochure, using the dashed lines as guides. Have them fold the right side first, so the left flap covers the right flap and opens toward the left like the cover of a book (figure 1).

figure 1

3. Then have students turn the brochure over and cut around the outline of the silhouette, making sure to cut through all three layers. The area where the arms attach to the dashed lines should not be cut. The brochure can now be opened, revealing a chain of three paper dolls.

Completing the Body Brochure

1. Invite students to use creative lettering to write a title on the cover flap. Then have them lift the cover flap to reveal two silhouettes. On the right one, ask students to draw the organs associated with the body system they researched—such as the heart, major arteries, and veins of the circulatory system, or the major bones of the skeletal system (figure 2).

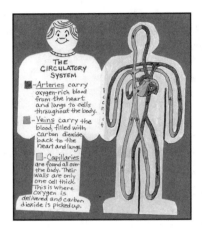

figure 2

2. Students can write about the system they researched on the three interior silhouettes. Encourage students to explore different reporting styles; they can define terms, illustrate body organs, create graphs, and so on (figure 3).

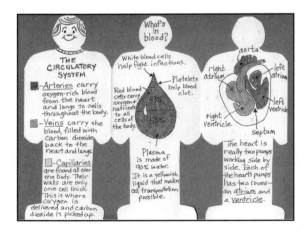

figure 3

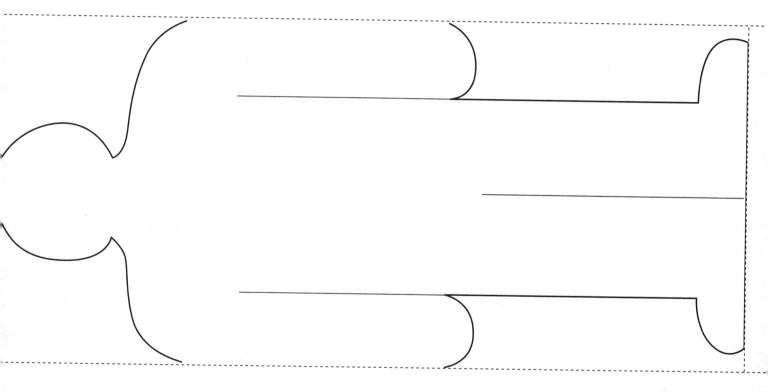

Data Disk 1

Materials:

- colored pencils
- scissors
- 8½- by 11-inch card stock
- glue sticks
- metal brads
- copies of the Data Disk template (page 34)

Skills/Standards:

- gathers and uses information for research purposes
- understands essential concepts about nutrition and diet
- knows how to maintain and promote personal health
- understands the fundamental concepts of growth and development

Teacher Tip

Data disks can be used in a variety of ways by changing the types of windows you cut out of the top disk.

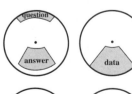

Purpose

Students will learn about foods in which the four basic nutrients—proteins, carbohydrates, fats, and vitamins and minerals—can be found.

Creating the Data Disk

1. Pass out a copy of the Data Disk template and two pieces of card stock to each student. Have students glue the template page onto a sheet of card stock.

2. Instruct students to cut out the perimeter of the template and use this disk to trace a circle onto the second sheet of card stock. Have students cut out this circle as well.

3. Ask students to cut out the two windows marked with the dashed lines on the template. Then have them place this on top of the second circle and fasten them together by pushing a metal brad through the center dot.

Completing the Data Disk

1. Ask students to write the word "Nutrients" above the top window and the word "Examples" below the bottom window, as shown in the sample project above. They should write their name on the left side of the disk and use creative lettering to write the title "You Are What You Eat" on the right side of the disk.

2. Ask students to write the word "Proteins" inside the top window. Beneath this word, still inside the window, they

should write a few facts about the importance of this nutrient. Inside the bottom window, have students draw several icons representing foods in which proteins are found (such as fish, eggs, milk, beans, and nuts).

3. Have students rotate the disk and write the word "Carbohydrates" and add a few facts in the top window. They should draw icons of carbohydrates in the bottom window.

4. Students should rotate the disk again and write about "Fats," then rotate the disk once more and write about "Vitamins and Minerals."

Physical Science

Students can use the two windows in the data disk to report on the boiling and freezing points of different elements, to compare the differences between sound waves and light waves, or to describe parallel and series circuits.

Earth Science

In the top window of the data disk, students can draw a picture of a landform; they can describe and define it in the bottom window.

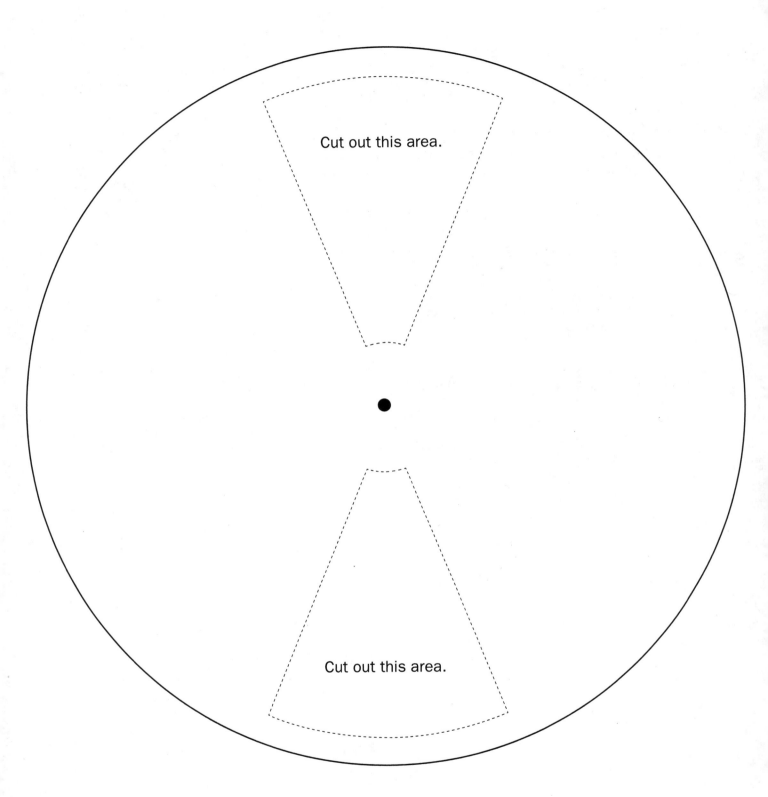

Cut out this area.

Cut out this area.

Four-Fold Book

Materials:
- colored pencils
- scissors
- Four-Fold Book template (page 37)

Skills/Standards:
- understands the scientific enterprise
- understands the cause and effect relationship between plate tectonics and changes in the Earth's surface

Teacher Tip

Many projects in this book, such as this one, can be glued directly into students' notebooks to make them even more interactive.

Purpose

Students will research and describe the different movements of the Earth's crust caused by plate tectonics.

Creating the Four-Fold Book

1. Pass out a copy of the Four-Fold Book template to each student. If your copier accepts paper larger than 8½ inches by 11 inches, enlarge the scale of the four-fold book to give students more room to write.

2. Have students cut out the cross shape and fold the bottom panel upward along the dashed line (figure 1). Then have them fold the right panel, left panel, and top panel along the dashed line so they overlap each other. (The photos of the sample project above show the project closed and fully open.)

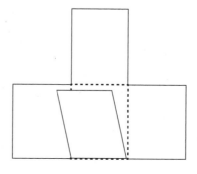

figure 1

Completing the Four-Fold Book

1. Invite students to use creative lettering to write the title "My Four-Fold Book of Plate Tectonics" on the front of the topmost panel.

2. Have students lift the top panel—Convergent Boundaries (Subducting). Ask them to color the square above the title red. On the blank panel opposite it, students should use a red-colored pencil to describe the cause and effect of this type of plate movement.

3. Ask students to lift the panel on which they just wrote to reveal another type of plate movement. Have them color the square above this title blue. On the blank panel opposite it, have students use a blue colored pencil to describe the cause and effect of this type of plate movement.

4. Have students use two other colors to code and describe the other two types of plate movements.

☐

Convergent Boundaries (Subducting)

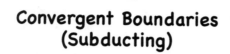

☐

Convergent Boundaries (Colliding)

☐

Divergent Boundaries

☐

Transform Boundaries

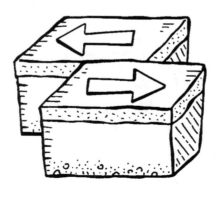

Circular Flap Book

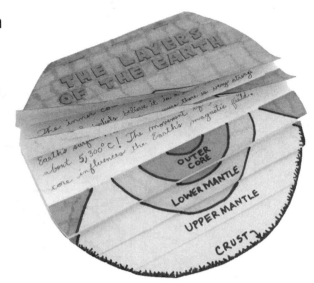

Materials:

- colored pencils
- pencils
- scissors
- compass
- stapler
- ruler
- 12- by 18-inch white construction paper

Skills/Standards:

- understands the nature of scientific inquiry
- gathers and uses information for research purposes
- collects and organizes information from multiple sources
- identifies the composition of the Earth's layers

Life Science

Students can also create a flap book that looks like figure 2 at right (not cut into a circular shape) that examines the layers of skin. The top panel can show the epidermis, and each succeeding flap can examine a deeper layer of skin tissue.

Purpose

Students will learn about the composition of the Earth and record their findings in a layered flap book shaped like the Earth.

Creating the Circular Flap Book

1. Pass out three sheets of 12- by 18-inch white construction paper to each student. Have students lay the sheets on top of each other so they are offset by 1¼ inches at the bottom (figure 1).

2. Show students how to bend the tops of the sheets backward (figure 3) to reveal panels 4, 5, and 6 (figure 2).

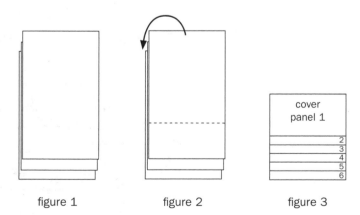

figure 1   figure 2   figure 3

3. Ask students to staple the flap book together with a single staple at the top center, then make a light pencil mark 4 inches down from the top center (figure 4).

4. Using a ruler as a guide, have students draw a line from the pencil mark to the bottom left corner of the flap book and another line from the pencil mark to the bottom right corner (figure 5).

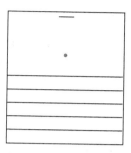

figure 4

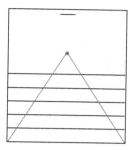

figure 5

5. Have students make a second light pencil mark 5½ inches down from the top center. With this pencil mark as a center point, ask students to use a compass to draw a circle with a 6½ inch diameter. The circle will touch the edge of the bottom panel but will go slightly beyond the two side panels and the top panel (figure 6). Have students cut out the circle and add more staples at the fold if needed.

6. Using the two diagonal lines as beginning and ending points, have students use the compass to draw four arcs that have diameters of 1¼ inches, 3 inches, 4 inches, and 6¼ inches, respectively (figure 7).

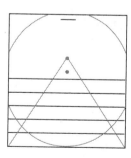

figure 6

figure 6

Earth Science

Ask students to study the layers of the Earth's atmosphere and report their findings in a circular flap book.

Completing the Circular Flap Book

1. Invite students to use creative lettering to write the title "The Layers of the Earth" on the top panel. On the five title strips below the cover, students should write the titles "Inner Core," "Outer Core," "Lower Mantle," "Upper Mantle," and "Crust," respectively.

2. Tell students to color the cover panel blue, the inner core red, the outer core orange, the lower mantle yellow-orange, the upper mantle yellow, and the crust brown.

3. Instruct students to lift the cover panel to reveal panel two and write information they learned about the inner core of the Earth. They should do the same for each of the other layers of the Earth that they studied.

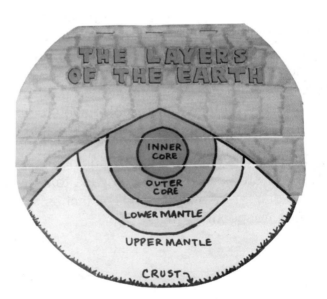

Circle Book

Materials:
- colored pencils
- scissors
- glue sticks
- Circle Book templates (pages 43–44)

Skills/Standards:
- understands the nature of scientific inquiry
- conducts research to find answers to questions
- organizes and interprets data
- understands cause-and-effect relationships
- understands how measurement tools are used to gather, analyze, and interpret data

Teacher Tip

Circle books can be made using any symmetrical design. Tailor the shape to the subject you're studying. For example, use a star or sun when studying space, a heart to report on the circulatory system, clouds to describe different cloud formations, or a flower when studying plant life.

Purpose

Students will research different kinds of natural disasters—their causes, how they are measured, scientists involved in their study, safety precautions that should be taken in response to them, and their historical significance.

Creating the Circle Book

1. After the class researches natural disasters, give each student one copy of the Drawing Sheet template on page 43 and three copies of the Writing Sheet template on page 44.

2. On the drawing template, let students create a title for their circle book—such as "My Circle Book of Hurricanes"—and draw a related illustration. On the writing templates, have students write about three aspects of the disaster—such as famous hurricanes of the past, where they typically occur, and how they are formed—and draw a picture in the area above the lines.

3. Ask students to cut out the four circles and fold them in half (figure 1).

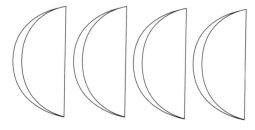

figure 1

Teacher Tip

Students can create circle books with as many as two dozen pages. Instead of gluing the last page to the first page, they can make a cover by gluing the first and last page to a sheet of poster board. (Secure the cover by squirting glue into the binding and setting it aside to dry.) You can display these by tacking the front and back covers to a bulletin board, allowing the pages to fan out. This is particularly effective when reporting on ecology or Earth science because the circular pages look like globes when they're attached to a bulletin board.

4. Instruct students to glue the right half of page 1 to the left half of page 2 (figure 2). Then have them glue the right half of page 2 to the left half of page 3 (figure 3), and the right half of page 3 to the left half of page 4. Finally, ask them to complete the circle book assembly by gluing the right half of page 4 to the left half of page 1.

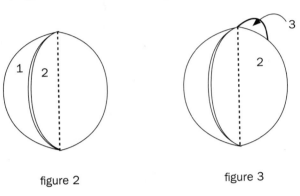

figure 2   figure 3

5. To display the circle books, hang a string across the classroom. Tie lengths of thread to the string, and then affix a paper clip to the ends of the thread. Attach the circle books to the paper clips and allow them to spin in the breeze.

Create a title for your circle book and draw a related illustration. Then fold the page in half along the dotted line. Reopen the page and cut out the circle.

Write about an aspect of the subject you studied and draw a related illustration in the space above the lines. Then fold the page in half along the dotted line. Reopen the page and cut out the circle.

Super Triorama

Materials:

- colored pencils
- glue sticks
- scissors
- tape
- colored construction paper
- 8½- by 14-inch white construction paper
- various craft materials

Skills/Standards:

- understands the nature of scientific inquiry
- knows that scientific investigations involve asking and answering questions and comparing the answer to what scientists already know
- collects and organizes information from multiple sources
- understands cause-and-effect relationships
- explores science concepts

Teacher Tip

Create an eye-catching display by gluing two trioramas side by side and then stapling them to a bulletin board. This type of display is great for reporting two-fold concepts like *before and after*, *cause and effect*, or *problem and solution*.

Purpose

Students will study the causes, effects, and solutions of different types of pollution and work in groups to create eye-catching, three-dimensional displays that illustrate what they learned.

Creating the Super Triorama

1. Break your class into groups of four and ask each group to study the causes, effects, and solutions of a different type of pollution.

2. Give each student a sheet of 8½- by 14-inch white construction paper. Ask them to fold the top left corner of the paper diagonally so that the top edge of the paper is flush with the right edge of the paper (figure 1).

3. Have students fold the top right corner diagonally so that it touches the lower point of the previous fold (figure 2).

4. Students should fold the rectangular panel at the bottom up so that a horizontal crease is made (figure 3).

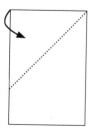

figure 1

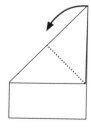

figure 2

figure 3

Earth Science

Students can work in cooperative groups to create super trioramas that depict different biomes as they appear throughout the four seasons.

Life Science

Highlight the similarities and differences of four animals that live in the same habitat.

5. Ask students to open up the paper to reveal four triangular quadrants and a flap. Have them cut the diagonal crease between quadrants 1 and 4 up to the center point of the quadrants (figure 4).

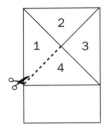

figure 4

Completing the Super Triorama

1. At this point, the groups need to decide on which aspect of pollution each member will report. One student will create a general scene that illustrates the type of pollution his or her group studied. A second student will illustrate one of the causes of this type of pollution; a third will spotlight an effect; and a fourth will depict a solution.

2. Have students draw the background of their scene across quadrants 2 and 3 (figure 5). Then have them draw the ground area of the scene on quadrant 1 (figure 6).

3. Ask students to pull point A over to point B so that quadrant 1 sits on top of quadrant 4. This will form the triorama display. Have students glue the base into place (figure 7).

4. Encourage students to use construction paper, string, cotton, markers, craft sticks, toothpicks, glue sticks, and other craft materials to create a scene that looks as three-dimensional as possible (see sample project on page 45).

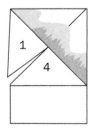
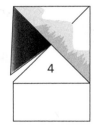
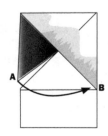

figure 5 figure 6 figure 7

5. On the panels below the scene, ask students to write a title for their scene—such as "Ozone Depletion," "Causes of Ozone Depletion," "Effects of Ozone Depletion," or "Solutions to Ozone Depletion"—followed by a descriptive paragraph (figure 8).

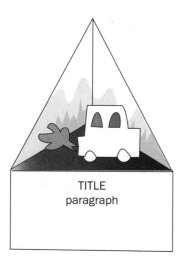

TITLE
paragraph

figure 8

6. When the four triorama displays are finished, glue them side by side to form a four-sided pyramid display. (See sample project on page 45.) The pyramids can be displayed on a table or counter top.

7. Encourage each group to give an oral presentation highlighting the information they learned. Discuss ways we can all be more responsible in helping prevent the pollution of our planet.

(See sample project on page 45.)

General Science

At the end of the school year, encourage your class to reflect on all they've learned and to create triorama displays of the topics they most enjoyed. Attach four students' trioramas together to construct "Pyramids of Science."

Pyramid Mobile

Materials:

- colored pencils or markers
- glue sticks
- scissors
- string
- hole punch
- paper clips
- 9- by 12-inch construction paper

Skills/Standards:

- understands the nature of scientific inquiry
- collects and organizes information from multiple sources
- understands the nature and composition of different types of rocks

Teacher Tip

To display the mobiles, hang a string across your classroom. Tie the mobiles to this string. When a breeze blows past the mobiles, they spin and create a vibrant display to jazz up the classroom!

Purpose

Students will compare characteristics of the three basic types of rocks, learn about their composition, and understand the major Earth processes that formed them.

Creating the Pyramid Mobile

1. Give each student a sheet of 9- by 12-inch construction paper. Show students how to fold the top left corner of the paper diagonally so that the top edge of the paper is flush with the right edge of the paper (figure 1).

2. Next, have students fold the top right corner diagonally so that it touches the lower point of the previous fold (figure 2), then cut off the rectangular panel at the bottom (figure 3).

3. Ask students to open up the paper to reveal four triangular quadrants. Have them cut the diagonal crease between quadrants 1 and 4 up to the center point of the quadrants. Students should then use a pair of scissors to snip a small hole in the center of the paper where the creases cross (figure 4).

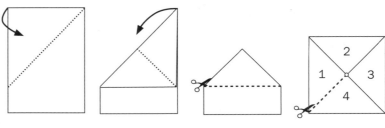

figure 1   figure 2   figure 3   figure 4

4. Invite students to use creative lettering to write the names of the three types of rocks—igneous, metamorphic, and sedimentary—in quadrants 1, 2, and 3 so the lettering faces the edge of the paper (figure 5).

5. Ask students to pull point A over to point B (figure 6) so that quadrant 1 sits on top of quadrant 4; the writing should be on the topside of the pyramid. Have students glue quadrant 1 on top of quadrant 4 (figure 7).

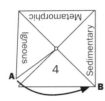

figure 5

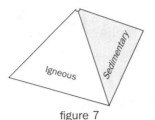

figure 6

figure 7

6. Ask students to punch a hole in the bottom center of each side of the pyramid, below the names of the types of rocks (figure 8).

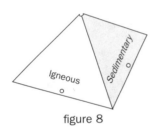

figure 8

Completing the Pyramid Mobile

1. Give each student a sheet of construction paper. Have students cut the sheet in half vertically and horizontally so they each have four pieces of paper. They should place one of the pieces in front of them horizontally and on it write the title "Types of Rocks." Then have students punch a hole in the top center of the paper and another hole in the bottom center of the paper.

2. Students should place a second piece of paper in front of them vertically and write facts about igneous rocks on it (how they are formed, their physical properties, where they can be found, and so on). Students can write facts on both

General Science

Pyramid mobiles are a great way for students to report on scientific concepts that can be found in "threes," such as the three branches of science.

Earth Science

Ask students to create a pyramid mobile that illustrates the three types of galaxies, the three parts of the water cycle, or the major layers of the Earth.

Physical Science

Students can create a pyramid mobile that examines the three basic states of matter, Newton's laws of motion, or the primary hues in white light.

sides of the paper. On the third piece, students can write facts about metamorphic rocks. They can write facts about sedimentary rocks on the last piece. Ask students to punch a hole in the top center of all three of these pieces of paper.

3. Give each student three 12-inch lengths of string and two 6-inch lengths of string. Ask students to tie one of the 12-inch lengths to the hole at the bottom-side of the pyramid that says "Igneous." They should tie the other end of this string to the card that contains facts about igneous rocks. Ask students to tie the fact cards for metamorphic and sedimentary rocks to their corresponding sides of the pyramid.

4. Ask students to tie one of the 6-inch lengths to a paper clip and thread it through the hole at the top of the pyramid so the paper clip rests on the underside of the pyramid and prevents the string from slipping through. Students should tie the other end of this string to the bottom of the "Types of Rocks" title panel. Have students tie the other 6-inch length to the top of this title panel.

Read-Around Report

Materials:
- colored pencils
- rulers
- scissors
- tape
- string
- paper clips
- hole punches
- thread
- Read-Around Report template (page 53)
- 9- by- 27-inch sheets of bulletin board paper

Skills/Standards:
- understands the nature of scientific inquiry
- understands cause-and-effect relationships
- explores the details of the water cycle

Purpose

Students will understand the repetitive steps involved in the water cycle—evaporation, condensation, and precipitation—and create a read-around report that documents their knowledge.

Creating the Read-Around Report

1. Give each student a sheet of 9- by 27-inch bulletin board paper and three copies of the Read-Around Report template.

2. On each of the three templates, ask students to draw a picture that depicts one of the three steps of the water cycle. Underneath the picture, have them write the name of the step depicted in the drawing followed by a descriptive paragraph. They should then cut out the three pictures along the edge of the frame.

3. Have students glue the drawing that depicts "Evaporation" one-half inch from the left edge of the bulletin board paper, the drawing that depicts "Precipitation" one-half inch from the right edge of the paper, and the drawing that depicts "Condensation" in the center of the paper (figure 1).

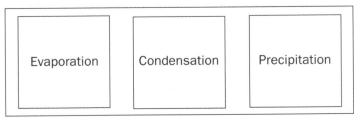

figure 1

Earth Science

Students can create read-around reports to describe the many cyclical processes found in nature, such as the four seasons, the phases of the moon, or the tidal cycle.

Life Science

Use read-around reports to explore the life cycle, metamorphosis, or the reproductive cycle of plants.

4. Ask students to curl the paper into a cylinder (with their drawings facing out) and tape it. Then show students how to punch four holes in the top of the report cylinder, tie strings to each of the holes, and connect those strings to a central string (figure 2).

Drawings on outer side.

figure 2

5. Suspend a long string across the classroom. Tie the read-around reports to this string so they can spin freely.

_____

_____

_____

_____

_____

Postcard Pocket Book

Materials:

- colored pencils
- rulers
- scissors
- tape
- glue sticks
- 12- by 18-inch sheets of construction paper
- 8½- by 11-inch sheets of white card stock

Skills/Standards:

- understands the nature of scientific knowledge
- gathers and organizes information for research purposes
- identifies traits, characteristics, and attributes of the planets in our solar system
- knows characteristics and movement patterns of the eight planets in our solar system (e.g., planets differ in size, composition, and surface features; some planets have moons, rings or particles, and other satellites orbiting them)

Purpose

Students will create postcards that highlight interesting facts about each of the planets in our solar system.

Creating the Postcard Pocket Book

1. Give each student two 12- by 18-inch sheets of construction paper and two 8½- by 11-inch sheets of card stock. Have students cut the two sheets of construction paper so they each measure 10 by 18 inches.

2. Ask students to place one sheet of construction paper in front of them horizontally and fold up the bottom 4 inches, creating a long pocket (figure 1). Repeat this with the second sheet.

figure 1

3. Have students tape the two ends of the pocket on each sheet closed (figure 2).

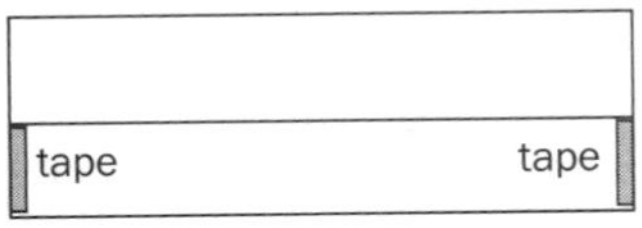

figure 2

General Science

Invite students to create historical postcards that spotlight major inventions from eight decades of the last century.

Earth Science

Students can imagine they've visited major landforms around the world and create postcards that describe their journeys. Or they can "time travel" to prehistoric eras and send postcards back to the future recounting things they saw.

4. Next, instruct students to fold both sheets in half so the pocket is on the outside (figure 3).

figure 3

5. Then have them fold the two sides in half so that the pocket is on the inside of the accordion cases (figure 4).

figure 4

6. Ask students to tape the back right edge of one accordion case to the back left edge of the second one, creating a large accordion case that has eight pockets (figure 5).

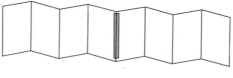

figure 5

7. Next, have students cut both sheets of card stock in half, vertically and horizontally, to make eight postcards.

Completing the Postcard Pocket Book

1. On each postcard, have students draw a picture of one of the eight planets, highlighting distinguishing features or interesting topographical characteristics. On the back of each card, encourage students to write a complete, detailed paragraph that describes the planet, its moons or satellites, the mythology behind its name, its date of discovery, its length of orbit, and so on.

Life Science

Students can create post-cards that highlight plant and animal life of different ecosystems. Or they can take microscopic journeys through the human body and send back postcards that highlight what they saw.

2. When students have finished the eight postcards, ask them to insert each card into one of the pockets of the accordion case—Mercury in the far left pocket, Neptune in the far right pocket. Students can write the name of each planet on the front of the corresponding pocket. Underneath the names, ask students to write a sentence using the initial consonants of each of the planets, such as *My Very Eager Mother Just Served Us Nachos,* to help them remember the order of the planets.

3. Encourage students to use creative lettering to write a title on the cover of the postcard pocket book.

Little Book

NEW MOON

The moon is between the earth and sun, so all we see is shadow.

Materials:

- scissors
- Little Book template (page 59)

Skills/Standards:

- understands the causes associated with changes in the moon's appearance
- identifies the eight phases of the moon
- enhances observation skills
- recognizes relationships regarding the relative positions of the sun, Earth, and moon
- develops critical thinking skills

Teacher Tip

Create a blank little book, write directions on each page, reopen the paper, and make copies. Pass out the template for students to complete. Little books are great to take on field trips, because they can fit in students' pockets and keep them focused on the task of completing the required information.

Purpose

Students will identify and describe the eight phases of the moon.

Creating the Little Book

1. Give each student a copy of the Little Book template. Have students fold it in half width-wise, with the writing on the outside (figure 1).

2. Instruct students to fold it in half in the same direction (figure 2), then fold the paper in half again in the opposite direction (figure 3)

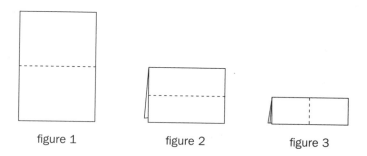

figure 1   figure 2   figure 3

3. Instruct students to unfold the paper to the position shown in figure 2 and cut halfway along the center fold (figure 4).

4. Have students unfold the paper completely. There should be a slit in the center of the paper where they made the cut (figure 5).

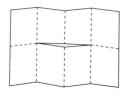

figure 4   figure 5

Earth Science

Students can make little books of Pangaea. They can sketch the super-continent on the first double-page spread, show the separation of the continental plates on the second double-page spread, and draw the continents as they appear today on the third double-page spread. Ask students to explain the theory of continental drift below each of the illustrations.

Physical Science

Students can draw and describe open, closed, series, and parallel circuits on each of the pages of a little book.

Life Science

Students can create a little book of bones that describes types of joints, the function of the skeletal system, or the composition of bones.

5. Have them fold the paper in half along the fold with the slit (figure 6). The writing should be visible on the outside.

6. Show students how to push in on the ends of the paper so the slit opens. Tell them to keep pushing until the center panels meet (figure 7).

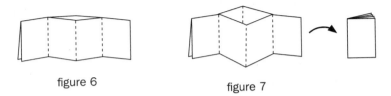

figure 6   figure 7

7. Finally, students can fold the pages to one side to form a little book and crease the edges. The cover should show the image of the new moon; if a different image is on their cover, students should flip through the little book and bend the spine so the image of the new moon is on the cover.

Completing the Little Book

1. As students research the eight phases of the moon, ask them to write information they learned on the lines below each of the illustrations. They can describe the positions of the Earth, moon, and sun; explain the effects of the moon's gravitational pull on the Earth's tides; explain the moon's orbit around the Earth; write about lunar eclipses; describe the lunar surface and topography; or recount stories of space missions to the moon.

WANING
CRESCENT

NEW
MOON

WAXING
CRESCENT

FIRST
QUARTER

THIRD
QUARTER

WANING
GIBBOUS

FULL
MOON

WAXING
GIBBOUS

Wall Display

Materials:
- colored pencils
- ruler
- 12- by 18-inch white construction paper

Skills/Standards:
- understands the nature of scientific inquiry
- collects and organizes information from multiple sources
- organizes and interprets data
- identifies traits, characteristics, or attributes of periodic elements
- conducts research to find answers to questions
- classifies things based on how they are alike

Teacher Tip

Look at a colored example of a periodic table and give students sheets of construction paper that color-coordinate the elements based on their chemical properties.

Purpose

Students will work together as a class to create a large wall display of the periodic table of elements.

Creating the Wall Display

1. Ask students to choose one or more elements from the periodic table. For each element they choose, give students a sheet of 12- by 18-inch white construction paper.

2. Have students place the paper in front of them vertically. Ask them to draw a line two inches from the bottom of the paper. Then have them fold the paper upward along this line (figure 1).

3. Instruct students to fold the top of the paper down and tuck it behind the bottom flap. It will look like a closed matchbook (figure 2).

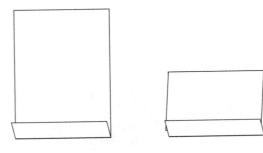

figure 1   figure 2

Completing the Wall Display

1. Have students write the name of the element they chose on the two-inch flap at the bottom. On the upper flap, students should write the chemical symbol and the atomic number of the element. (See the sample project on page 60.)

2. Ask students to lift the upper flap. Have students print out a picture from the Internet of a product that uses the element or is made from the element. Have them glue the picture on the upper panel. Next to the picture, students can write a sentence describing how the element is used in the product.

3. On the lower panel, have students write a paragraph about how the element fits into the periodic table, its characteristics and attributes, its natural state, who discovered the element and when, and other related information.

4. When the class is finished, hang the projects on a wall—reflecting the order of their atomic numbers—to create a large display of the periodic table of elements. Students can refer to it as they learn more about the chemical composition of the world around us.

Earth Science

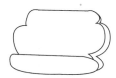

Students can cut the edges of the displays so they look like clouds and use them to report on different types of cloud formations. Add the reports to a background of blue bulletin board paper, so it looks like a cloud-filled sky.

Life Science

During a unit on botany, students could create a wall display that focuses on different types of flowers or trees. Or after a field trip to the zoo, students could create displays of their favorite animals.

Flip-Flop Book

Materials:

- colored pencils
- white construction paper
- scissors
- glue sticks
- Flip-Flop Book template
  (page 63)

Skills/Standards:

- understands the nature of scientific inquiry
- collects and organizes information from multiple sources
- explores mixtures and solutions
- investigates how substances react chemically with other substances to form new substances
- understands relationships in scientific formulas

Teacher Tip

To create a flip-flop book with more than four panels, tape two books together to create an eight-panel book. Students can then define additional terms, such as heterogeneous mixture, homogeneous mixture, suspension, and colloid.

Purpose

Students will define and identify examples of elements, compounds, solutions, and mixtures.

Creating the Flip-Flop Book

1. Give each student a copy of the Flip-Flop Book template. Have students glue the template to a sheet of white construction paper. (This step is optional, but it keeps the writing from showing through the cover flaps and gives the project a more finished look.)

2. Have students cut each of the dashed lines on their templates, making sure to stop where the dashed line meets the solid line. Ask them to fold the flaps down so that the writing lines are on the inside of the fold.

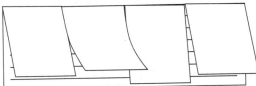

Completing the Flip-Flop Book

1. The flip-flop book now has four panels. Invite students to use creative lettering on the cover of each panel to write the words "Element," "Compound," "Solution," and "Mixture." Instruct students to draw an icon below each word that will help them remember the meaning of each term.

2. Have students lift the four flaps. In the upper area inside each panel, have students write a definition of the term on the flap's cover. In the lower area, have them fill in some examples of the term.

Top Tab Book

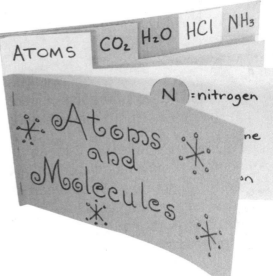

Materials:

- colored pencils
- scissors
- liquid glue
- toothpicks
- black marker
- stapler
- 12- by 9-inch sheets of construction paper
- Atoms and Molecules template (page 67)

Skills/Standards:

- develops critical thinking skills
- understands the nature of scientific knowledge
- understands the structure and properties of molecules
- knows that matter is made up of atoms
- knows that atoms often combine to form a molecule, the smallest particle of a substance that retains its properties

Teacher Tip

Vary the number and size of the pages to meet the needs of the subject you're studying.

Purpose

Students will construct simple models of atoms and molecules to help them understand that different atoms can combine in different ways to form many kinds of molecules.

Creating the Top Tab Book

1. Give each student three 12- by 9-inch sheets of light-colored construction paper. Ask students to cut the sheets in half to create six sheets that measure 9 by 6 inches (figure 1). Have students set one of these sheets aside; we'll call this panel F.

2. Instruct students to place one of the sheets horizontally in front of them and draw a line 1¼ inches down from the top (figure 2). Then ask students to draw a vertical line 1½ inches from the right edge of the paper, stopping at the horizontal line they just drew. Have students draw three other lines, 3 inches, 4½ inches, and 6 inches from the right edge of the paper (figure 3). We'll call this panel A.

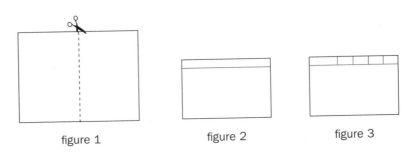

figure 1   figure 2   figure 3

3. Tell students to set one of the sheets aside; this will be panel F. Then have students place panel A on top of another sheet. Have them cut away the top right (first) rectangle on both sheets (figure 4) to create panel E. Have students place panel E to the side on top of panel F.

4. Have students create the rest of the tabs in a similar fashion. Ask them to place panel A on top of another sheet and to cut away the length of the first and second rectangles on both sheets (figure 5) to create panel D. Students should place panel D on top of panel E.

5. Instruct students to place panel A on top of another sheet and to cut away the length of the first, second, and third rectangles on both sheets (figure 6) to create panel C. Students should place panel C on top of panel D.

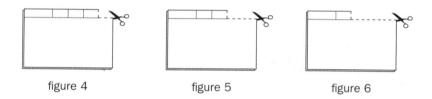

figure 4   figure 5   figure 6

6. Have students place panel A on top of the last sheet. Tell them to cut away the length of the first, second, third, and fourth rectangles on both sheets (figure 7) to create panel B. Tell students to place panel B on top of panel C.

7. Finally, have students cut away the rest of the top strip on panel A and place this panel on top of the other five panels (lining it up with the bottom edge). They can staple together the left edges of all six panels to create a Top Tab Book (figure 8).

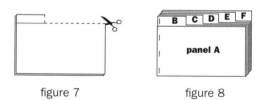

figure 7   figure 8

Earth Science

Students can use extra large construction paper to create a four-page top tab scrapbook that focuses on the four seasons.

Encourage students to create a seven-page top tab diary to track their eating and exercise habits over the course of a week.

Completing the Top Tab Book

1. Invite students to use creative lettering to write the title "Atoms and Molecules" across the cover of panel A.

2. Ask them to write the title "Atoms" on the top tab of panel B. Then give students a copy of the Atoms and Molecules template. Have them cut out six circles from the template, write the chemical symbol of the six different elements within the circles, and color the circles according to the key that appears on the template page. Next, instruct students to glue the six circles to panel B and write the name of each element next to the corresponding atom (figure 9). This will serve as the color key for the molecules the students will be creating on panels C through F.

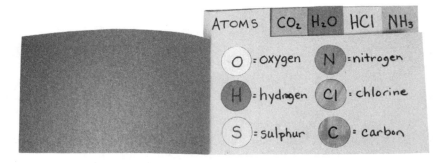

figure 9

3. Finally, have students choose four of the molecules listed on the template and write the chemical formula of those molecules on the top tabs of panels C through F (one formula per tab). Using toothpicks to represent chemical bonds between atoms, students will glue the toothpicks and color-coded atoms to the corresponding panels to illustrate the different molecules (figure 10). They should write the name of the molecule above the model.

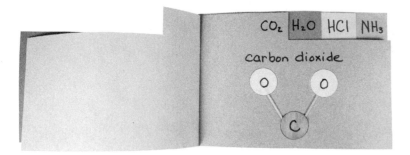

figure 10

Template   Atoms and Molecules

ATOM KEY		
ATOMIC ELEMENT	**SYMBOL**	**COLOR**
Carbon	C	Blue
Chlorine	Cl	Green
Hydrogen	H	Red
Nitrogen	N	Orange
Oxygen	O	White
Sulphur	S	Yellow

MOLECULE KEY	
MOLECULE	**FORMULA**
Water	H_2O
Carbon Dioxide	CO_2
Nitrogen Dioxide	NO_2
Sulfur Dioxide	SO_2
Hydrochloric Acid	HCl
Ammonia	NH_3

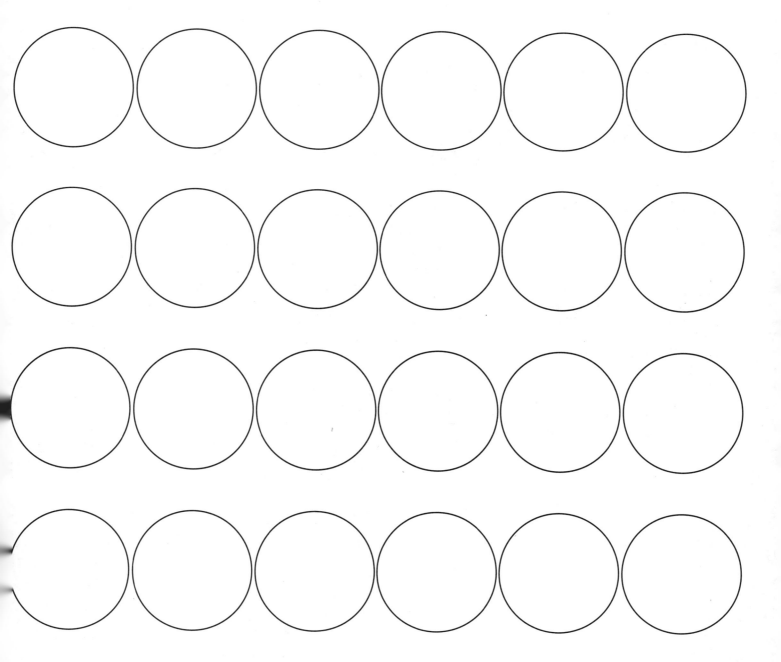

KWL Desktop Display

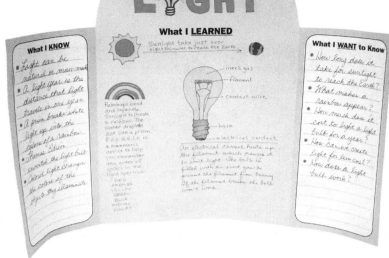

Materials:

- colored pencils
- scissors
- glue sticks
- ruler
- 18- by 12-inch sheets of construction paper
- KWL Writing Sheet template (page 70)

Skills/Standards:

- understands the nature of scientific inquiry
- activates prior knowledge about a topic
- generates questions about a topic
- gathers and uses information for research purposes
- knows that scientific investigations involve asking questions and comparing the answer to what scientists already know
- organizes and interprets data

Purpose

Students will create a trifold display about light and sound that is small enough to fit on a desktop but large enough to include plenty of important information they learned about the subject.

Creating the Desktop Display

1. Give each student an 18- by 12-inch sheet of light-colored construction paper. Ask them to lay the paper horizontally in front of them and make a small pencil mark 4½ inches from the left side. Using the pencil mark as their guide, have students fold the left edge toward the center of the paper, creating a 4½-inch panel (figure 1).

2. Have students fold the right edge toward the center so it abuts the left-hand panel (figure 2).

3. Ask students to draw a light pencil line 2½ inches from the top, across both folded panels. Instruct students to cut away the area above the lines on the two folded panels. This allows the center panel to be rise above the side panels. Ask students to round off the top corners of the center panel (figure 3).

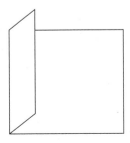

figure 1

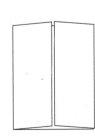

figure 2

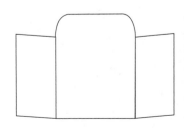

figure 3

Completing the Desktop Display

1. Create a list of topics related to light and sound that you would like the class to explore. Ask each student to pick a topic from the list.

2. Give each student a copy of the KWL Writing template. On the What I Know section, ask students to write several sentences describing things they already know about the topic they will research. Have them cut this section out and glue it to the inside left panel of the desktop display.

3. On the What I Want to Know section, ask students to write several sentences describing things they would like to learn about the topic they will research. Have them cut this section out and glue it to the inside right panel of the desktop display.

4. Invite students to use creative lettering to write a title for the desktop display at the top of the center panel. Below the title, instruct students to write the words *What I Learned.* After students have researched a topic, encourage them to write paragraphs, draw diagrams, and create charts that explain things they've learned. Ask them to glue their findings on the center panel of the desktop display. Remind students to include a list of the sources they used in their research.

5. Finally, encourage students to report their findings to the class. Line up the displays on a counter top for everyone to enjoy.

Physical Science

The desktop display is reversible, so you can have students write about light on one side and sound on the other.

Teacher Tip

If students need more space to report their findings, they can glue the What I Know and What a Want to Know paragraphs on the outer sides of the two side panels. This allows students to devote all three inner panels to the information they learned in their research.

Template **KWL Writing Sheet**

What I **KNOW**	What I **WANT** to Know

Laptop Web Page

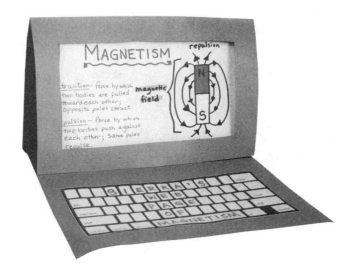

Materials:

- colored pencils
- rulers
- scissors
- glue sticks
- highlighters
- 18- by 12-inch sheets of construction paper
- Web Pages template (page 74)
- Keyboard template (page 75)

Skills/Standards:

- understands the nature of scientific inquiry
- collects and organizes information from Internet Web sites
- organizes and interprets data
- develops critical thinking skills
- makes connections between data related to science concepts

Purpose

Students will explore various aspects of magnetism and create four mock-up Web pages that link ideas and concepts together.

Creating the Laptop Web Page

1. Give each student two 18- by 12-inch sheets of colored construction paper. Have them cut off 2½ inches from the width of both sheets, so they each measure 18 by 9½ inches.

2. Have students lay one of the sheets in front of them horizontally. Ask them to draw lines that are 6 inches, 12 inches, and 15 inches from the left edge (figure 1). In the figure below, the four quadrants are marked A, B, C, and D.

3. Ask students to draw a 1-inch border around quadrant B. Then have them cut out the area within the border to create a window (figure 2).

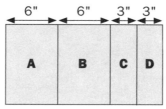

figure 1

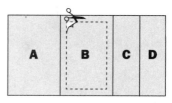

figure 2

Students can create a Web site that features pages that delve deeper and deeper into the layers of the Earth or further and further back in time through important geologic eras.

4. Have students fold quadrant A over quadrant B and quadrant D over quadrant C (figure 3). Then have them fold quadrant CD over quadrant AB (figure 4).

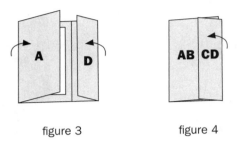

figure 3   figure 4

5. Ask students to open up the paper, put glue on the inner side of quadrant D, and attach quadrant D to the outer side of quadrant A (figure 5). This will create the triangular laptop monitor as shown in the photograph on page 71.

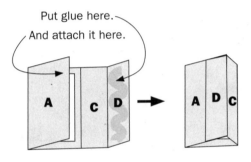

figure 5

6. Instruct students to cut the second sheet of construction paper in half, so each piece measures 9½ by 9 inches. (They will only use one of these sheets.) This sheet will serve as the base of the laptop keyboard. Have students rub glue on the bottom of the laptop monitor (quadrant C) and attach it to this sheet of paper (figure 6).

figure 6

Completing the Laptop Web Page

1. Pass out two copies of the Web Pages template to each student. Have them cut the templates in half along the dashed line. Students will design four Web pages that delve further into the subject of magnetism. The first page they design will be the home page. It should include general information about the topic they researched. Ask students to use a highlighter to emphasize one of the sentences or concepts on the home page.

2. The second Web page will explore the concept they highlighted on the home page in more detail. Encourage students to draw illustrations, create charts, or write paragraphs that further explain the highlighted concept. Then ask students to use a highlighter to emphasize something on the second Web page. (The third Web page will explore the concept highlighted on the second page. The fourth page will explore the concept highlighted on the third page.)

3. Have students insert the four Web pages into the side of the monitor so the home page can be seen through the window. Each page can be pulled out and then reinserted behind the other three pages so the viewer can learn more about magnetism.

4. Finally, pass out a copy of the Keyboard template. Ask students to create a title for the laptop Web page by writing letters on the keys. (See finished project on page 71.) Have students cut out the keyboard and glue it onto the panel below the monitor.

Life Science

Invite students to explore the layers of the rain forest. Each Web page can focus on the animal and plantlife that can be found in each layer.

Template Keyboard

Write the title of your Web page on the computer keys.
Cut out the keyboard and glue it onto your laptop.

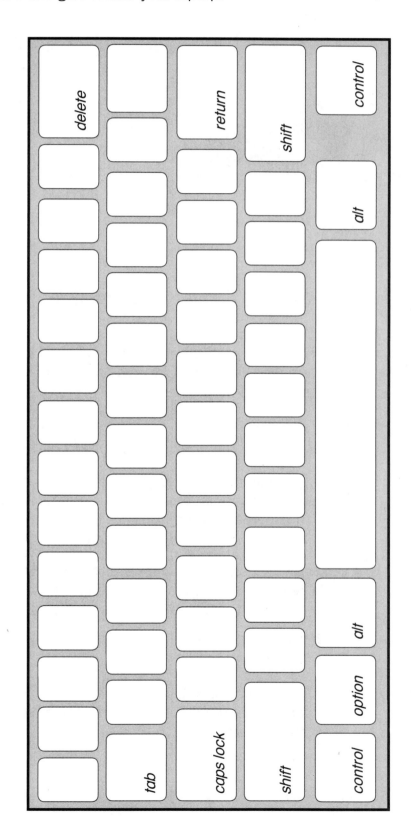

Comic Strip

Materials:
- colored pencils
- scissors
- tape
- ruler
- Comic Strip Panels template (page 77)

Skills/Standards:
- understands the nature of scientific knowledge
- conducts research to find answers to questions
- explores a science concept
- develops critical-thinking skills
- understands the benefits and disadvantages of using alternate forms of energy

Life Science

Students can create comic strips that illustrate ways in which the body's immune system fights infections or how fruits and vegetables keep the human body healthy.

Purpose

Students will research forms of alternative energy, design a superhero who represents the powerful benefits of an alternative energy source, and create a comic strip that features this character.

Directions

1. Have students research a form of alternative energy and make a list of its benefits. Then invite them to design a superhero that represents the energy source and devise a scenario in which the superhero helps save the day.

2. Give all students a copy of the Comic Strip Panels template. Ask them to cut along the dotted lines and tape the four panels into one long strip.

3. Tell students to draw the superhero and write a title for the comic strip in panel 1.

4. Then, in panels 2, 3, and 4, students will illustrate an energy-related problem that is solved by the superhero they created.

Template Comic Strip Panels

panel 2

panel 3

panel 1

panel 4

Data Disk 2

Materials:
- colored pencils
- scissors
- 8½- by 11-inch card stock
- glue sticks
- metal brads
- Data Disk templates (pages 79 and 80)

Skills/Standards:
- understands the nature of scientific inquiry
- understands the scientific method
- plans, conducts, and documents a simple experiment

Teacher Tip

Create an extra large data disk out of two sheets of poster board to document an experiment the whole class performed.

Purpose

Students will conduct an experiment and create a data disk that documents their learning about the steps of the scientific method.

Creating the Data Disk

1. Give each student two sheets of card stock and a copy of the Data Disk A and Data Disk B templates. Instruct students to glue both disks to a sheet of card stock and cut them out. They should also cut out the viewing window on Disk A.

2. Have students place Disk A on top of Disk B. Then show them how to fasten the disks together by pushing a metal brad through the black dot in the center of Disk A.

Completing the Data Disk

1. Encourage students to add a title and illustration to the front of the disk that relates to an experiment they will perform.

2. Ask students to write information about the five steps of the scientific method in the viewing window, rotating the disk to write about each step. They can list the materials needed for the experiment on the back of the disk.

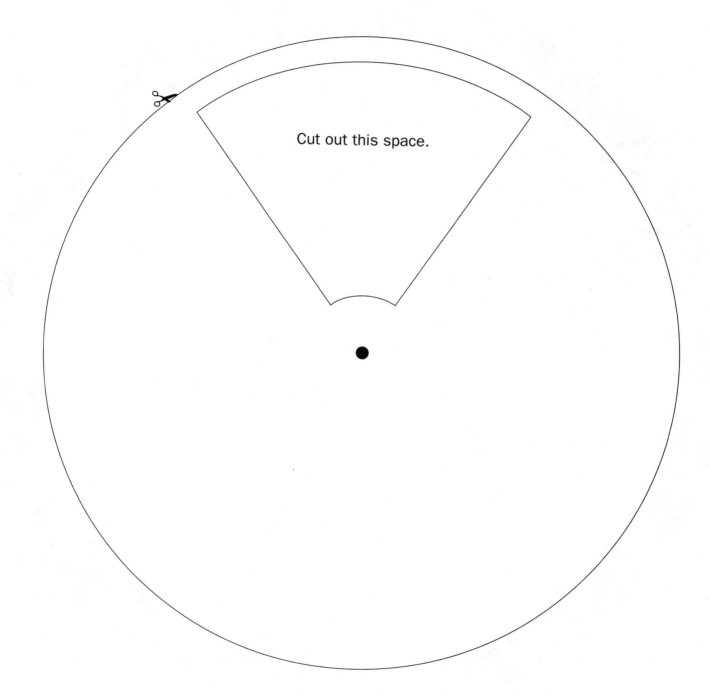

Cut out this space.

1. RESEARCH QUESTION

2. HYPOTHESIS

3. PROCEDURE

4. DATA

5. CONCLUSION

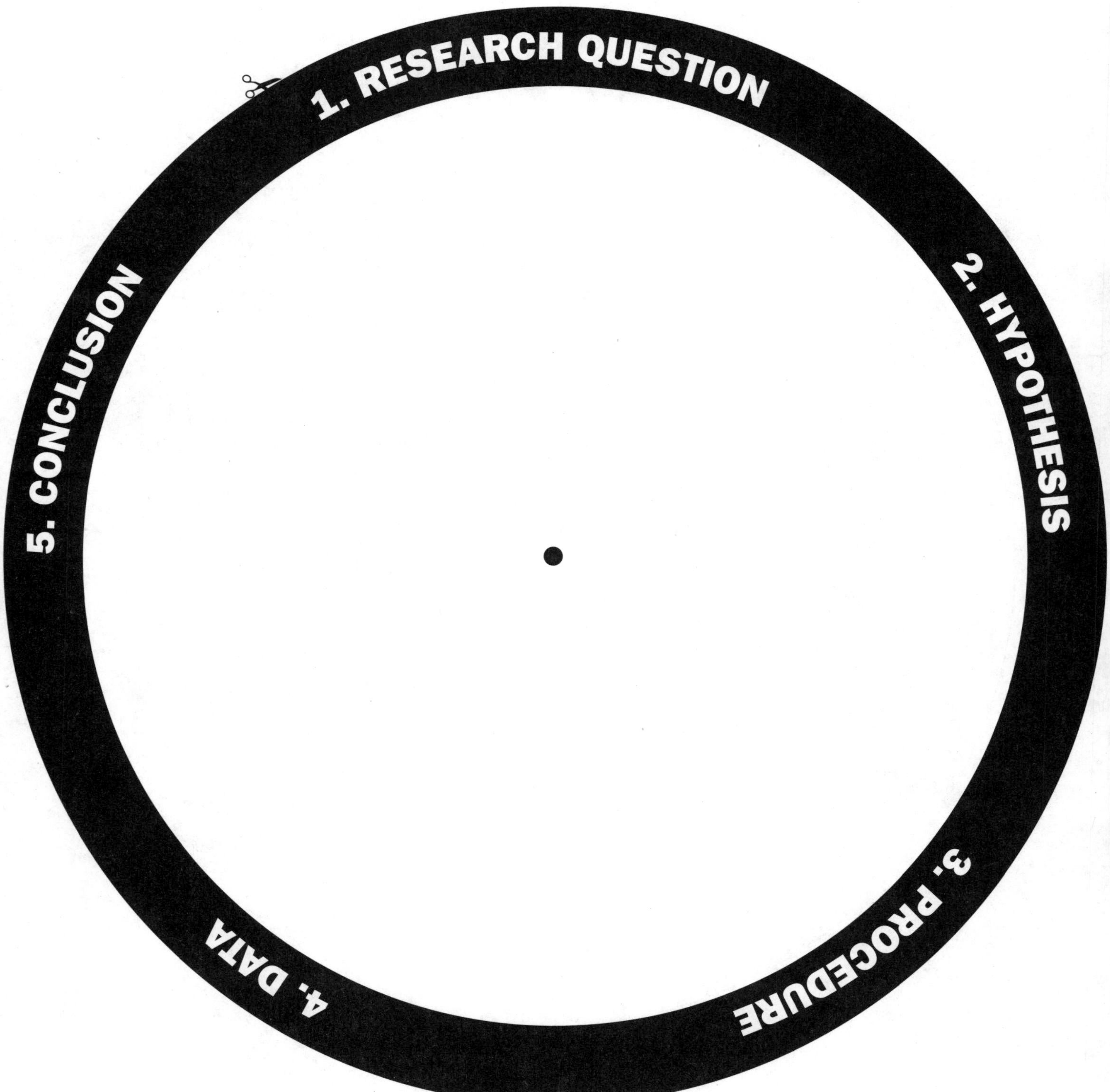